BIBLE STORIES FOR LITTLE CHILDREN

VOLUME TWO, REVISED EDITION

Danny

by Betty R. Hollender

illustrated by Lee Bearson

UNION OF AMERICAN HEBREW CONGREGATIONS
New York, New York

IN LOVING MEMORY
GRANDPARENTS OF LITTLE CHILDREN
FRIEDA and LOUIS
SALLY and CHARLES

Library of Congress Cataloging-in-Publication Data
(Revised for vol. 2)

Hollender, Betty R.
  Bible stories for little children.

  An illustrated retelling of the stories found in the
Old Testament.
  1. Bible stories, English—O.T. 2. Bible stories—
O.T. I. Bearson, Lee, ill. II. Title.
BS551.2.H6 1986   221.9'505   85-24708

Publication of this book was made possible
by a generous grant from the
GRANCELL FAMILY FOUNDATION

INTRODUCTION

Stories from the Bible are a rich source of Jewish literacy and identity. No wonder, then, that Jews of all ages tell and retell stories of the matriarchs, patriarchs, kings, and prophets.

Children love stories. And what better gift can we give to our sons and daughters than the treasure of Scripture, made accessible to them at precisely the moment they begin to read. In bringing biblical characters to life, in presenting them with all their strengths and all their shortcomings, in emphasizing the values that their lives embodied, we say to our children: You, too, can be a Jewish leader. You, too, can make a difference.

For some three decades, Betty Hollender's *Bible Stories for Little Children* has been read and enjoyed by hundreds of thousands of young people. Now recast in a more contemporary style, Ms. Hollender's stories will enable the study of the Bible for yet another generation.

We are proud to bring this special volume to you, and we hope that it will be widely used in both classrooms and homes throughout North America.

Rabbi Daniel B. Syme

THANK YOU

I wish to thank all the people who made this book possible. Their enthusiasm as well as their contributions have made it a special volume.

Some of these people are: Rabbi Daniel B. Syme, Rabbi Howard I. Bogot, Stuart L. Benick, Aron Hirt-Manheimer, Annette Abramson, and Lee Bearson, the artist, for his wonderful illustrations.

Thanks also go to my husband, Herbert, who has been an inspiration for all my creative efforts.

Betty R. Hollender

CONTENTS

BE STRONG AND OF GOOD COURAGE

Moses was a great leader.
He took the Jews out of Egypt.
He taught them the Ten Commandments.
He led them for forty years in the hot desert.

One day, he called Joshua to him.
"Joshua," he said, "I am old.
I have led my people for many years.
They need a new leader now.
They need a young leader to take them
into the Promised Land.
They need you.
Do not be afraid.
God will help you.
God will help you lead your people
across the Jordan River and into the Promised Land."
Then Moses went up to the top of a mountain,
and no one ever saw him again.

One night, Joshua sat in his tent.
He was thinking about the Promised Land.
"Babies, girls, mothers, and grandmothers;
boys, fathers, and grandfathers;
tents, flocks, weapons; our Holy Ark, too—
all must cross the Jordan.
I can get them across the Jordan.
I can keep them dry and safe.
But what will happen on the other side of the river?

"People live in the Promised Land.
Will they be friends or enemies?
Will they fight us?
Or will they welcome us and help us to live
at peace in the land?

"I wish Moses were here.
He would tell me what to do," thought Joshua.
And then Joshua remembered.
He remembered Moses blessing him.
He remembered Moses saying, "Be strong. Be brave.
Remember God is always with you."

"God is always with you," said Joshua to himself.
"God was with Abraham and Sarah,
and Abraham and Sarah had a son.
God was with Joseph,
and Joseph saved his family.
God was with Moses,
and Moses led us out of Egypt.
God was with us in the desert,
and we received the Ten Commandments.
God is with us now, and we will cross the Jordan
and make our homes in the Promised Land."

THE WALLS CAME TUMBLING DOWN

So the Jews lived in the Promised Land.
They built homes.
They planted gardens.
They had children.
"We like this land," said the children.
"But how did you find it?"
"God brought us here," answered the mothers.
"God brought us here, but we had to fight to stay,"
said the fathers.
Listen, and we will tell you the story.
But remember, we were not there.
Our parents told us the story.
Our grandparents told it to them.
Our great-grandparents told it to them.
This is how they remembered it.

Many people lived in the Promised Land then.
Some people were friends.
They helped the Jews build homes.
They gave the Jews seeds to plant in their gardens.
They welcomed the Jews to live with them
in the Promised Land.

Other people said, "We do not want the Jews here.
We have strong cities.
They cannot capture our cities.
We will fight the Jews.
Then they will go away."
Jericho was a city.
But it did not look like a city.
Around the city were very strong walls, very high walls.
The city looked more like a fort.

"We do not want the Jews to live in the Promised Land.
We have a strong city.
We have brave soldiers.
We will fight the Jews.
We will conquer them.
Then they will go away."
Joshua called the Jews together.
"All roads lead to Jericho," he said.
"The people of Jericho do not want us to live here.
We must capture Jericho, or we cannot stay.
God has promised us this land.
But we must work to get it.
Who will help?"

"I will help," someone called.
"I will help, too," called another.
"We will all help," called all the people together.
"Good," said Joshua.
"Everyone will have a job.
Listen and I will tell each of you what to do.

"Old men!
You guard the camp.
Young men!
You take weapons.
Priests!
You carry the Holy Ark.
Seven priests bring *shofarot.*
You will need them when we get to Jericho.

"Young men and priests, follow me.
Do not make a sound.
Watch me carefully.

At the walls of Jericho, I will raise my hand.
The priests will blow their *shofarot,*
but the soldiers will be very quiet.
I will lead you.
And we will go around the walls of Jericho.
Then we will march back to camp.

"Forward, forward, follow me.
Follow me to victory."
Joshua stopped speaking.
The army went forward, forward to Jericho.
First came Joshua, brave and strong.
Next his soldiers marched along.
The priests marched behind the soldiers.
They held God's Ark.
More soldiers followed the priests.
The army marched quietly to Jericho.

At Jericho, priests sounded the *shofarot;*
soldiers marched around the city.
Then the priests stopped blowing.
They put down their *shofarot,*
and Joshua's army marched away.

Six days Joshua and his army marched around Jericho.
On the seventh day, the army marched to Jericho
again.
Around and around and around the city
marched Joshua's army.
The walls were very high.
The walls looked very strong.
But Joshua's soldiers were brave.
"God will surely help us," they said.

Around and around and around the city
went Joshua's soldiers.
They marched around Jericho seven times.
Then Joshua cried, "Shout for *Adonai*, our God!"

The soldiers shouted.
The priests blew their *shofarot*.
And the walls came tumbling down.

"Did the walls really tumble down?"
asked the children.
"We do not know," answered their parents.
"We were not there.
Our parents were not there.
Our grandparents were not there.
Our great-grandparents were not there, either.
But this is the story their parents told them
when they asked,
'How did we come to this pleasant land?'"

LOVE YOUR GOD

One day, Joshua called the Hebrews together.
"I am getting too old to be your leader," he said.
"You need a young leader now.
But first, I have something important to tell you.

"Always remember *Adonai*, our God,
who brought us out of Egypt,
kept us alive in the desert, gave us the Ten
Commandments, and found us a home in the
Promised Land.

"Remember we promised to love *Adonai*, our God,
to keep the commandments, and to
worship only *Adonai*.
Remember this promise, and you will be happy;
forget it, and you will be sad."
"We will remember," promised the Hebrews.
"We will remember our promise to God."

And they meant to remember.
But sometimes they forgot.
Sometimes they worshiped the gods of their
neighbors, idols of wood or stone.

If one god did not help them, they worshiped another.
They forgot that *Adonai* had helped them.
They forgot that *Adonai* could help them.
They had fights with their neighbors,
and they were unhappy.

DOWN WITH BAAL

The Hebrews built homes in the Promised Land.
They planted corn and wheat.
The wheat grew.
They cut the wheat.
They ground it into flour for bread.
They were happy in the Promised Land.

But they forgot their God.
They forgot they had been slaves in Egypt.
They forgot Moses who brought them
the Ten Commandments.
And they forgot that they had wandered in the desert
before they came into the Promised Land.

They forgot their God.
They prayed to the god of their neighbors.
They prayed to Baal, the god of the Midianites.

But did Baal help them?
Not at all.
Baal could not keep the Hebrews safe from harm.
He was only an idol made of stone.

The Midianites fought the Hebrews.
And the Midianites won.
They set fire to the Hebrews' wheat.
They stole the wheat that did not burn.

"Our God has forgotten us," cried the people.
But did they pray to their God?
No!

They forgot God.
They went right on praying to Baal.

Gideon was the youngest son of a poor Hebrew farmer.
One day, Gideon was cutting his wheat.
"I will hide this wheat," he said.
"The Midianites must not find it.
It is too bad that I must hide it.
Our God promised us this land.
Now God lets our enemies burn our wheat.
Are my friends right?
Has God forgotten us?" thought Gideon to himself.
"Or have we forgotten God?

"We pray to Baal.
We do not pray to God.
God can help us.
Baal cannot.
Abraham and Sarah knew that God would help them.
God gave them a son.
Joseph knew that God would help him.
God saved Joseph's family from famine.
Moses knew that God would help him.
God led the Hebrews out of Egypt.
I know that God will help us now.
And I must show everyone that this is so.

"How shall I begin?

"The altar to Baal—I will smash it down.
I will build an altar to *Adonai*, the Living God,
in place of the altar to Baal.
I will do it tonight."

That night, Gideon went to the village square.
He smashed Baal's altar.
He built an altar to the Living God in its place.

In the morning, the people came to the village square.
They did not see the altar to Baal.
But they did see the altar to *Adonai*, the Living God.

"Who threw down Baal's altar?" they asked.
"I threw it down," said Gideon.
"Baal cannot help you,
but *Adonai*, the Living God, can.
The Midianites burn your crops.
Baal does not stop them.
The Midianites steal your wheat.
Can an idol get it back for you?
The Midianites fight you,
and they win all the battles.
Baal cannot help you.
Adonai, the Living God, can.

"God helped Abraham, Isaac, and Jacob.
God helped Sarah, Rebecca, Rachel, and Leah.
God helped Joseph, Moses, and Joshua.
Now God will help us.

"Down with Baal!
Whoever is for God, follow me.
We will beat the Midianites.
And we will be happy in our land once again."

"Down with Baal!" called the people.
"Victory with *Adonai* and Gideon."

HORNS AND PITCHERS

The people followed Gideon to a brook.
Gideon stopped at the brook.
He turned around.
"We have plenty of men to fight the Midianites,"
said Gideon.
"We need some men to raise wheat and corn.
We need some men to help the women and children.
And we need some to take care of the camp
when we go out to fight.

"Everyone, go and take a drink from the brook.
We will see who will be the best soldiers.
We will see who will make the best farmers
and guards."

Everyone in the group took a drink.
Some lapped up water with their tongues.
Some kneeled down to get their water.
And some made cups of their hands;
filled the cups with water;
and drank the water that way.

Gideon watched the people drink their water.
"The people who made cups of their hands
will be my soldiers," he said.
"The others will take care of our farms.
They will help around camp
and guard the women and children."

Gideon and his soldiers set up their camp.
The other people went home.

The next day, Gideon called his soldiers together.
"Tonight we attack," he said.
"Each soldier will carry a horn.
And each soldier will carry a pitcher.
Inside the pitcher will be a candle.
The candle will be lit.
Carry the pitcher carefully
so the candle does not go out.

"I will divide you into three groups.
The three groups will surround the Midianite camp
on three sides.
When I blow my horn, you blow your horn.
When I smash my pitcher, you smash your pitcher.
When I hold my lighted candle high,
you hold your lighted candle high, too.
Then we will all shout,
'For *Adonai* and for Gideon.'
And you will see what will happen."

That night, Gideon's soldiers
surrounded the Midianite camp.
They blew their horns.
They smashed their pitchers.
They held their candles high,
and they shouted, "For *Adonai* and for Gideon."

The Midianites were surprised.
The Midianites were frightened.
They were so frightened they did not fight at all.
They did not know what to do.
So they ran.
They ran as fast as they could.
They tried to get away from Gideon's soldiers.
But they could not run fast enough.

Gideon's soldiers followed them, crying,
"For *Adonai* and for Gideon."

SAMSON'S SECRET

The Philistines were neighbors of the Hebrews.
The Philistines were not friendly.
They burned fields.
They stole sheep.
They fought with the Hebrews all the time.
But the Philistines were afraid of one Hebrew.
Who do you think he was?

A farmer's son?

A man with long hair?

A very strong man?

You are right.
The man was Samson.
Samson was a farmer's son.
Samson had long hair.
Samson was one of the strongest people
that ever lived.

He killed a lion with his bare hands.
He broke heavy ropes.
He pulled up the gates of a city,
put them on his shoulders, and carried them away.
Everyone knew Samson was strong,
but no one knew why.

The Philistines feared Samson
so the Hebrews made him their leader.
"What makes Samson so strong?" asked one Philistine.
"That is Samson's secret," said another.
"He will never tell you why he is so strong," said a third.

"No," said the first Philistine,
"Samson will never tell why he is so strong.
But I know someone who can help us find out."
"You do?" asked the second.
"Who is it?" asked the third.

"Delilah," answered the first.
"Samson loves Delilah.
He will tell her anything,
anything she wants to know."
"Let us ask Delilah," said the others.

They found Delilah.
"Find out why Samson is strong," they said.
"We will give you 1,100 pieces of silver."
"I will ask him," said Delilah.
"I will find out why Samson is so strong."

That night, Delilah said to Samson,
"Samson, I love you.
You are the strongest man I know.
Tell me your secret.
What makes you so strong?"
"Take new bowstrings and bind me," said Samson.
"Then I will not be strong.
I will not be able to break the bowstrings."
"This will be easy," thought Delilah.
"Soon I shall have my money."

Samson fell asleep.
Delilah bound him.
"Come in, Philistines," called Delilah.
"Look at Samson.
He is not strong anymore."

In came the Philistines.
"Samson, Samson, the Philistines are upon you,"
called Delilah.

Samson woke up.
He broke the bowstrings.
He rushed at the Philistines.
The Philistines ran away.
Delilah began to cry.
"Samson, Samson, you do not love me.
You did not tell me the truth," cried Delilah.

"I do love you," said Samson.
"I love you very much.
I will tell you my secret now.
Bind me with new ropes,
and I will not be strong anymore."
"I will bind Samson with new ropes," thought Delilah,
"then I will get my money."

Samson fell asleep.
Delilah bound him with new ropes.
"Come in, Philistines," called Delilah.
"Come and see Samson now."
In came the Philistines.
"Samson, Samson," called Delilah.
"The Philistines are upon you."

Up jumped Samson.
He broke the ropes.
He rushed at the Philistines.
The Philistines ran away.
Delilah began to cry.
"Samson, Samson, you did not tell me the truth.

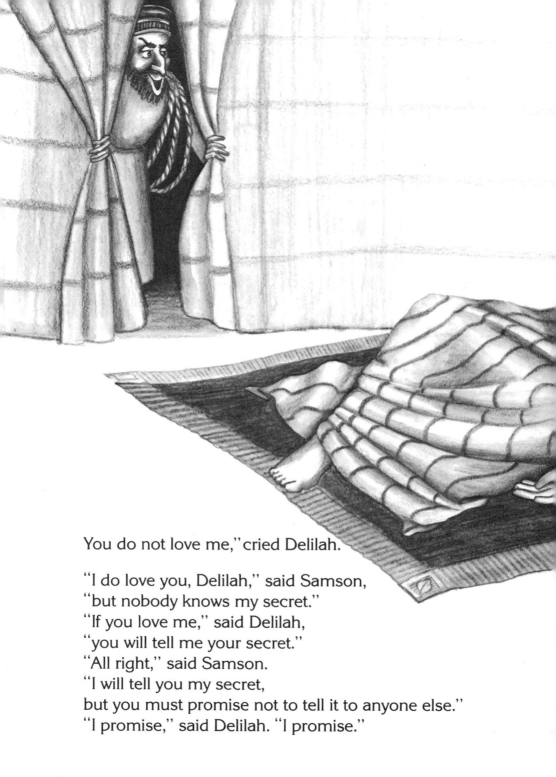

You do not love me," cried Delilah.

"I do love you, Delilah," said Samson,
"but nobody knows my secret."
"If you love me," said Delilah,
"you will tell me your secret."
"All right," said Samson.
"I will tell you my secret,
but you must promise not to tell it to anyone else."
"I promise," said Delilah. "I promise."

"I made a promise to God," said Samson.
"I promised to do God's work.
I never shave, and I never cut my hair,
to remind me of my promise.
I know, if I remember my promise, God will help me be
the strongest person in the world."

That night, Samson fell asleep,
and Delilah cut his hair.

Then she called, "Come in, Philistines;
Samson is not strong anymore."
In came the Philistines.
"Samson, Samson, the Philistines are upon you,"
cried Delilah.

Samson got up.
The Philistines grabbed him.
They bound him with ropes.
Samson tried to break the ropes,
but he could not do it.
He touched his head.
"My hair," cried Samson.
"You have cut it!

"I forgot my promise.
I wish I had remembered it.
God will not help me now."
Samson was not strong anymore.
He could not break the ropes.

The Philistines took him.
They put out his eyes.
He could not see.
They took him to prison.
They made him grind corn.
Round and round went Samson.
He dragged the millstone around and around
as he ground the corn for the Philistines.

Slowly, slowly, something began to happen.
Samson's hair began to grow.
First it was fuzz...very, very short.

Then it grew longer.
Samson's hair touched his ears.
"My hair," he thought, "it is growing long.
I remember my promise to God.
Maybe God will help me."
Samson's hair touched his shoulders.
"Wonderful," thought Samson.
"I am growing strong again,
and the Philistines do not know it.
They only know that I cannot see.
I must find a way to make those Philistines pay
for the trick they played on me.

"O God, help me," prayed Samson.
"I will always remember You.
Help me and make me strong."

A PHILISTINE HOLIDAY

Samson was in jail.
Around and around he went,
grinding corn for the Philistines.
He heard shouts.
He heard laughing.
He heard many people in the streets.
"Today must be a holiday," thought Samson.
"It must be the holiday of Dagon."

The Philistines were in their temple.
It was the holiday of Dagon, their god.

The Philistines thanked Dagon
for giving Samson to them.
They were very happy.
They were having a good time.
"It is too bad Samson is not here,"
said one Philistine.
"Yes," said another, "it is too bad
that Samson is not here. Poor Samson.
He drags that millstone around and around all day.
He never has a holiday.
He should be here with us.
We could have fun with him.

"We could tease him.
And he could not do anything about it.
We could laugh at him,
but he would not be strong enough to fight us."
"Yes, yes!" shouted the others.
"Let us bring Samson here.
It will be fun to tease him."

They sent a boy to get Samson.
"Come with me," said the boy.
"They want you at the temple."
"Why do they want me?" asked Samson.
"I do not know," said the boy.
"The Philistines think I am still weak,"
thought Samson.
"They do not know *Adonai* is with me.
I will show them how weak I am!
Now I will teach them a lesson,
and they will not forget it."

The boy led Samson into the temple.
"Boy," said Samson. "I am tired.
I want to lean against a pillar."
"Put your hand here," said the boy.
Samson put out his hand.
The boy took it.
He put Samson's hand on the pillar.
Samson felt with his other hand.
He wanted to find another pillar.
But all he felt was the air.

Samson felt with his hand again.
Still he did not feel the pillar.
Then he felt something hard.
"I have found it," thought Samson.
"I have found the other pillar."
Samson put his hand around it.
"I am holding two pillars," he thought.
Then Samson began to pray.
"O God, remember me, and strengthen me once more.
Let me punish the Philistines for fighting with my people."

Slowly, slowly, Samson pulled his hands together.
Crash went the pillars.
Crash went the temple.
Samson's strength had come back.
The Philistines did learn a lesson.
They did not bother the Hebrews for many years.

SAMUEL, LEADER OF ISRAEL

When Samuel grew up,
he became the leader of the Hebrews.
Samuel was not a soldier,
but he had to fight the Philistines anyway.
The Philistines grew stronger and stronger.
They burned fields.
They captured towns.
They even brought their idols to the Land of Israel.
They built homes and worshiped their idols
in the Land of Israel.
Many of the Hebrews forgot their God.
And they worshiped the idols, too.

Samuel did not like this.
He called the people together.
"Why do you worship idols?" asked Samuel.
"Can they make you well if you are sick?
Can they make the grass grow or the flowers bloom?
Can they make the sun shine or the wind howl?
Can they feed you when you are hungry?
Can they comfort you when you are sad?"

"No," someone said.
"No," said another.
"No! No! No!" called all the Hebrews at once.
"Idols are made of wood and stone.
How can they make the sun shine?
How can they send us food?
How can they make us well when we are sick?
How can they make us happy when we are sad?"

"Right!" said Samuel.
"Some idols are made of wood.
Some idols are made of stone.
They cannot move as you do.
They cannot speak as you do.
They cannot do many things you can do.

"But *Adonai* can do everything.
Adonai is all powerful.
Adonai is everywhere.
Adonai sees everything you do.
Adonai even sees that you worship idols.
Adonai does not want you to worship idols.
Worship *Adonai*, our God; *Adonai* will help you
and save you from the Philistines.
You will live in peace again.

"Let us pray together.
Say this prayer with me:

O God, we have forgotten You.
O God, we are sorry that we have forgotten You.
Forgive us we pray.
And we will never forget You again."

The Philistines saw that the Hebrews were listening
to Samuel.
"This is a good time to attack the Hebrews,"
they said.
"We will easily win."
As Samuel finished his prayer,
the Philistines attacked the Hebrews.
"Samuel, Samuel, what shall we do?"
cried the Hebrews.

"Have faith," said Samuel quietly.
"First let us pray.
Then we will fight."
Samuel prayed to God.
The people prayed with him.

The Philistines came nearer and nearer.
Suddenly thunder thundered.
Lightning flashed.
Rain came down, down, down.
The rain wet the Philistines.
Down, down, down it came.

It flooded their camp.
Down, down, down it came.
It wet their clothes.
Down, down, down it came
until their shoes were full of water.

Slosh, slosh, slosh!
The Philistines tried to run away.
But the Hebrews were too quick.
They ran after the Philistines.
They caught them;
they fought them;
they won the battle.

The Hebrews lived in peace again.
The Philistines did not bother them.
And Samuel was a judge in Israel all his life.

WE WANT A KING!

"We want a king. We want a king,"
shouted the people.
"Why?" asked Samuel.
"Why do you want a king?
You are happy now.
You have lived in peace for many years.
You have your own land.
You have your own cattle.
You have lived happily with your own families.
You are free to do as you want.
God is your King.
What can a human king do for you?"

"We want a king like other kings.
We want a king with a golden crown.
We want a king to tell us what to do,"
answered the people.

"You are lucky," said Samuel,
"but you do not know it.
Your neighbors have kings.
They must give money so their kings
may eat from golden plates.
They must give their sons so their kings
may have large armies.
They must give their daughters so their kings
may have cooks and dancers.

"But you can spend your money as you wish.
You can have your families around you.
You are free.
A king will give you orders,
and you will not be free."

"We want a king anyway," shouted the people.
"You have been a good leader, Samuel,
but you are getting old.
There is no one as wise as you to teach us God's ways.
What will we do when you are too tired to lead us?
What will we do then?
We will need a king to help us.
We will need a king to lead us.
We will need a king to fight for us."

"A king can lead you.
A king can fight for you.
A king can help you—but only if he follows God.
If you really want a king, I shall find one for you."

THE LOST DONKEYS

Samuel sat down in front of his house.
"I will watch the sunset," he thought.
"I will look down from the top of this hill.
I will see the trees and flowers that God has made.
I will see a city and its people that God has made.
I will enjoy the quietness and the beautiful sunset
that God has made, too."

Samuel looked down the hill.
A small, black spot was climbing up the hill.
The spot grew bigger and bigger.
Samuel saw that it was not a spot.
It was a young man.

The young man climbed to the top of the hill.
"Good evening," he said.
"Please tell me where I can find the house of Samuel,
the man of God."

"I am Samuel, the man of God.
Come with me to my house.
You shall eat with me there,
and you shall sleep there, too.
In the morning, you shall go on your way again."

"How do you know me?" asked Saul.
"We have never met.
You do not know my family."
"It is true," said Samuel.
"We have never met,
but I know something more about you.

You are looking for some donkeys.
Look no longer.
Your father has found them."

"You must be very wise," said Saul.
"You know so many things."
"Come with me now," said Samuel.
"Eat and sleep at my house.
In the morning, we will talk."

Saul did not sleep very well that night.
He tossed and turned.
He thought and thought.
"What will Samuel say to me?
What does he want me to do?
I am only a Benjaminite—the smallest tribe
in Israel.
And my family is small and not well known."

In the morning, Samuel called, "Wake up Saul.
It is time to go."
Up jumped Saul.
He dressed and ate.
Samuel went with him to the end of the city.
"Before you go," said Samuel, "stand still
and hear the word of God."
Saul stood very still.
"What will Samuel say?" he wondered.

"Why did he choose me?
Why did he choose me to hear the word of God?"
Samuel took out a horn full of oil.
He put some on Saul's head.

"Saul," he said, "God has chosen you
to lead our people in God's ways.
God has chosen you to be the first king of Israel.
If you follow God, you will lead your people well."

A KING FOR ISRAEL

Samuel called the people together.
"*Adonai* has saved you many times.
Adonai brought you out of Egypt,
helped you in the desert,
brought you to this land,
and helped you make homes here.
Still you are not happy.
You say, 'Only a king will make us happy.'
Let us find one now.

"Each tribe will come before me.
I will find you a king."

Saul heard Samuel's words.
He was afraid.
"I do not know what a king should do," he thought.
He ran away and hid.
He hid near the donkeys and carts.
He saw the tribes come before Samuel:
Judah, Reuben, Issachar, Zebulun, and Dan.
Simeon, Ephraim, Manasseh, Gad, Asher, Naphtali,
and, last of all, Benjamin.

"These are all good people," thought Samuel.
"But where is Saul?"
"God has chosen Saul to be your king," said Samuel.
"Where is he?"

Saul made himself as small as he could.
He hid behind a cart.
Saul saw the people looking for him.
But he did not come out.

"I am not good enough to be king," he thought.
"To be king of all of Israel."
The people looked for Saul.
Soon some of them found him.
"Come, Saul," they said.
"Samuel wants you.
God has chosen you to be our king."

"But I am not important," said Saul.
"I am just a human being like you, or you.
How can I be king over all Israel?"
"Go to Samuel," said the people.
"He will tell you what to do."

Saul was still afraid.
But he wanted to be king.
"I will surely make mistakes," he thought.
"A king should never make mistakes.
What will I do then?"
Saul followed the people to Samuel.
"Here is the one whom God has chosen," said Samuel.

"Do not be afraid, Saul," he said.
"Trust in God and obey the commandments.
God will help you always."
"Long live King Saul," cried the people.
"Long live King Saul."
"I will do my best," said Saul.
"I will trust in God, and I will protect my people."

FOOD FOR DAVID'S BROTHERS

"I wish I were a soldier, a soldier brave and tall.
I wish I were a soldier fighting for King Saul,"
sang David.

David's brothers were fighting.
They were fighting for King Saul.
They were fighting against the Philistines.
David was too young to be a soldier.
He had to stay home.
He stayed home and took care of his father's sheep.

"I can fight," said David to himself.
"My brothers are good fighters,
and I'm a good fighter, too.
And, if I were a soldier, I know what I would do.

"I'd take my sling...
fit a smooth stone into it...
whirl it round and round...
and...WHAAAM—

"I'd hit a Philistine right between the eyes.
I'd take another stone...
fit it into the sling again...
whirl it round and round...
and...WHAAAM—
Another Philistine would fall.

"But here I am.
I am not a soldier.
I am not near the fighting.
I cannot hear the fighting.

I live far away from King Saul's army.
My brothers are fighting for King Saul,
but I must watch my father's sheep.
I must keep them together.
I must keep them safe from wild animals.
I kill mountain lions to save the sheep.
I can kill Philistines, too."

The sun was going down.
"It is time to take the sheep home," thought David.
He got the sheep together.
One by one they followed him.
They followed David to his father's house.
David put the sheep in their pen.

"Hello, David," said his father.
"Are the sheep in their pen?"
"Yes, father," said David proudly.
"Every single sheep is in the pen.
Not one lamb was lost today.
They are all safe in their pen."
"That is fine," said his father.
"And now, I have something special to ask you.

"I have some food for your brothers.
Will you take it to them?"
"Will I?" said David.
"Certainly! I will start tomorrow morning."

The next morning David packed the food.
He took his sling, too.
"I'll need my sling," thought David.
"I might meet a mountain lion.
Good-by, father," he called.

Away went David to find his brothers.
Away went David singing his song.
"I wish I were a soldier, a soldier brave and tall.
I wish I were a soldier, fighting for King Saul."

43

TALLER THAN THE TREETOPS

Bumpity, bump, bump, went David and his donkey.
"I wish I were a soldier, a soldier brave and tall.
I wish I were a soldier, fighting for King Saul,"
sang David.

Bumpity, bump, bump, went David and his donkey,
down the road to King Saul's camp
with food for his brothers.

David and his donkey came to camp.
Saul's army was getting ready
to attack the Philistines.
Suddenly a roaring sound shook the trees.
Was it a mountain lion?
No. It was not a mountain lion.
Was it a bear?
No. It was not a bear.
Again, there was a roar.
Again, it shook the trees.
Then everything was quiet.

The soldiers stopped talking.
They stopped lining up for battle.
They stopped getting their spears ready.
They stood still and listened.
Then David looked.
What do you think he saw?
He saw a giant, tall as a tree.
The giant's spear was so heavy
that he needed two men to carry it for him.
And in back of the giant
was the whole Philistine army.

The giant came forward.
"What kind of soldiers are you?" he roared.
"Do you need a whole army to fight the Philistines?

"I am Goliath.
Send someone to fight me.
And we shall see who wins....
If your person kills me, you win.
If I kill that person, we win.
Send someone to fight—
one person who is not afraid of Goliath,
if you can find one."

No one answered Goliath.
He turned around.
He walked back to the Philistine camp.
"What is the matter?" asked David.
"Why will no one fight Goliath?"

"No one wants to fight someone as tall as a tree,"
said one soldier.
"No one wants to fight a giant
whose voice shakes the trees," said another.
"No one wants to fight a giant
whose spear is so heavy that
two men must carry it,"
said a third.

"I wish I were a soldier," said David.
"I wish I could fight Goliath.
I have killed mountain lions and bears,
chased wild animals back to their lairs.
Even a giant as tall as a tree
is not big enough to frighten me."

"You!" said a voice behind David.
"What are you doing here?
You should be with your sheep."
David turned around.
He saw his oldest brother, Eliab.
"I can fight Goliath," said David.
"You are too young to fight," said Eliab.
"You do not know how soldiers fight.
King Saul will never let you fight Goliath.
He knows you are only a boy."

"I've killed mountain lions and bears,
chased wild animals back to their lairs,"
said David.
"When they bother my sheep, I go after them,
grab them by the mane,
and kill them.
And I can kill the giant Goliath, too.
Please let me ask King Saul.
Please, Eliab."
"Very well," said Eliab.
"We will go to the king.
But do not be too excited.
The king may say no."

SWEET MUSIC FOR KING SAUL

David and Eliab hurried to the king's tent.
"Who goes there?" asked the guard.
"The sons of Jesse," said Eliab.
"We wish to see King Saul."
"The king is cross and restless.
He cannot sleep.
He will not see anyone," said the guard.
"Let me play the harp for him.
My music will put him to sleep," said David.

"I remember you," said the guard.
"King Saul once sent to Bethlehem for you.
He brought you here.
You played for him.
And he fell asleep.
Perhaps you could help him now.
I will ask Prince Jonathan."

The guard went into the tent.
Soon he came out with a harp.
"Here," he said.
"You may play this harp."

David went into the tent.
King Saul was tossing and turning.
He could not sleep.
David sat down.
He touched the harpstring and began to play.

He sang softly.
The king stopped tossing.
He stopped turning.

He fell asleep.
"David has soothed the king.
Look! He sleeps," whispered Jonathan.
"The king sleeps," whispered everyone in the tent.

David filled the tent with sweet music.
He played and played until the king woke up.
"Who plays that music?" he asked.
"I play it," said David.
"Your music has soothed me and put me to sleep.
You chased my worries away," said the king.
"What can I do to repay you?"

"Only one thing, let me fight Goliath," said David.
"Fight Goliath?" asked King Saul.
"My brave soldiers will not fight Goliath.
My generals will not fight him either.
You are only a boy.
You certainly cannot fight him."

"I have killed mountain lions and bears,
chased wild animals back to their lairs.
Even a giant tall as a tree
is not big enough to frighten me."

"Very well," said the king.
"I can see that you want to fight Goliath very much.
You may go.
You may fight the giant.
But be careful.
I shall want you to play sweet music for me again."

THE SLING THAT SAVED ISRAEL

David walked out of the king's tent.
Down, down the hill he walked.
Prince Jonathan followed David.
Eliab followed Jonathan.
And Saul's army watched.

At the bottom of the hill, David stopped.
He stopped to look at the brook
which was at the bottom of the hill.

He bent down.
He picked up some stones from the brook.
"One, two, three, four, five," he counted.
"These stones are not too little.
They are not too big.
They are just the right size for me to use."
He put the stones in his bag.
He walked back up the hill.
Jonathan followed David.
Eliab followed Jonathan.
And Saul's army watched.

"I would not like to be David," said one soldier.
"The giant Goliath is taller than the treetops."
"I would not like to be David," said another.
"Goliath's voice is so strong, it shakes the trees."
"And I would not like to be David," said a third.
"Goliath's spear is so heavy that it takes two men
to carry it."

David stood on top of the hill.
He could see the whole Philistine army.

He could see Goliath, too.
Goliath looked frightening.
But David was not afraid.
"The soldiers are afraid of Goliath," thought David.
"But I am not afraid of him.
God has helped me kill lions and bears,
chase wild animals back to their lairs.
Even a giant tall as a tree
is not big enough to frighten me."

Suddenly a loud voice roared and shook the treetops.
It was the voice of Goliath.
"Who dares to come out and fight?" roared the voice.
"Who dares to fight me?"
"I dare to fight you, Goliath," answered David.
"What? Does Saul send a boy to fight a giant?"
called Goliath.
"I will show you how a boy can fight,"
David called back.
"I will fight for the army of *Adonai*, the Living God.
God will help me.
And I will win the battle."

"Very well," roared Goliath.
"Are you ready?"
"Ready," answered David.

He fitted a stone into his sling.
Around and around it whirled.
Away it went. It hit Goliath in the forehead.
He fell over backwards.
David ran over to Goliath.
He took the giant's sword and killed him.

"God has helped me kill lions and bears,
chase wild animals back to their lairs.
And Goliath, the giant, has lost his last fight,
to a boy who was helped by the Living God's might,"
sang David.

All Israel sang, too.
The people were happy that Goliath was dead.
They were happy that they had won their battle.
"David is a sweet singer," they said.
"And David is a good fighter, too.
He has saved his people from the Philistines."

JONATHAN SAVES DAVID'S LIFE

"Saul has killed his thousands,
but David has killed his ten thousands,"
sang the Hebrews.
Saul heard them sing.
He was angry.
"I am the king," said Saul.
"I have won many battles.
I saved my people from the Philistines, too.
They must remember this.

"Jonathan, Jonathan," called Saul.
"Where is David? Find him.
Bring him back to me.
I want to see him."
"Why are you angry with David?" asked Jonathan.
"He fights battles to help you.
He plays his harp when you cannot sleep.
His music makes you feel quiet and good.
Why are you angry with him?"

"It is true," said Saul.
"David's music does make me feel good.
It puts me to sleep when I toss and turn.
But I have killed many Philistines,
and the people do not remember.
David kills a giant, and the people think only of David.
It makes me very, very angry,
especially when I don't feel well.
Go and get him, I say.
I must speak to him."

Jonathan went to find David.
He went out into the fields.
He knew David was hiding from the king.
David had heard the people sing.
He knew Saul was angry with him.
He knew Saul did not feel well.
So he hid in the fields.

Jonathan found David behind a large rock.
"You must go away, my friend," said Jonathan.
"My father, the king, is sick again.
He is very, very angry.
He has heard the people sing:
'Saul has killed his thousands,
but David has killed his ten thousands.'
He thinks you cannot be his friend.
He does not know that you love him.
You must go now.
Do not wait.
When my father is well again,
when my father understands
that you are his friend,
you can come back once more."

"You have been very kind," said David.
"Maybe I will be able to help you some day.
"It is nothing," said Jonathan.
"You have been a good friend to me.
And I have been your good friend.
You can always count on me to help you.
Good-by, David."
"Good-by, Jonathan."

Jonathan watched David go away.
He watched David get smaller and smaller and smaller.
He watched until he could not see David any more.

DAVID SAVES HIS ENEMY

Saul was angry at David.
Every place David went, Saul followed.
David hid in a city; an old friend hid him.
Saul and his soldiers followed.
David hid in the wilderness.
He ate berries and the meat of wild animals.
And all the time, Saul followed him.
"I will catch David," said Saul.
"He cannot escape from me."

One night, Saul camped near David's hiding place.
David saw him make camp.
But Saul did not see David.
When the sun went down, Saul went to sleep.
His soldiers went to sleep, too.

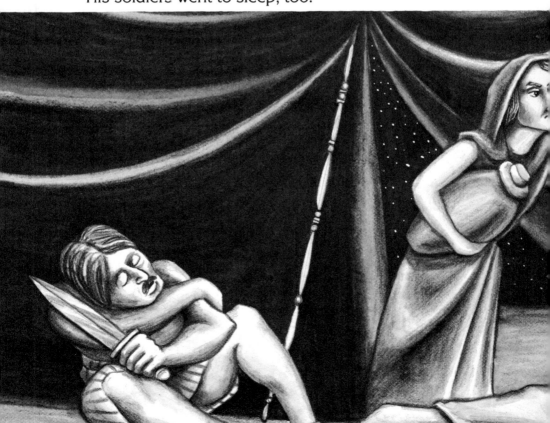

Everyone in Saul's camp went to sleep
except the guards.
"What a good chance for me," thought David.
"Come Abishai, my friend,
we will go into Saul's camp."
"What will we do there?" asked Abishai.
"We shall see," said David.

David and Abishai waited.
They waited till the guard was not looking.
They crept into Saul's camp.
Soon they found his tent.
The king was asleep.
Abner, the king's bodyguard, was asleep, too.
"Look, Saul's spear," whispered Abishai.
"It is sticking in the ground, next to him. See it?
Let me take it.

Let me kill Saul with his own spear."
"No," said David.
"God gives life, and God takes life.
Saul's day will come.
We must not kill him.
Come, we must hurry.
You take the spear,
I will take the water jar near his head.
Let us go."

Out of the camp crept David.
Out of the camp crept Abishai.
Up a hill they went—
up, up, up the hill they climbed.
At the top of the hill, David and Abishai stopped.
They faced Saul's camp.
"Abner, Abner," called David.
"Wake up!
You are brave.
You are a good fighter.
And you are a good watcher, too.
Why did you fall asleep tonight?
Where is the king's spear?
Where is his water jar?"

Abner woke up.
He rubbed his eyes.
He tried to see.
It was too dark.
He felt for the spear.
It was not there.
He felt for the water jar.
He could not feel that either.

"Abner, Abner," called David again.
"Where is the king's spear?
And where is his water jar?"

Saul woke up.
"That voice is the voice of David," he thought.
"Is this your voice, my enemy David?" called Saul.
"Yes," said David.
"This is the voice of David.
Why do you follow me, Saul?
Why do you wish me harm?
I have your spear, but I did not kill you.
I have your water jar, but I did not harm you.
What have I done to you?
Why do you call me 'enemy'?"

"You have my spear, but you did not kill me.
You have my water jar, but you did not harm me.
David, my son, I am sorry," called Saul.
"I have made a mistake.
Come back and live with me as you used to do."

"No," said David.
"Let one of your young soldiers come.
Let him get your spear," called David.
"And let him get your water jug, too.
I put my trust in God who will keep me safe.
God gave you to me today, but I would not kill
the king that God has chosen."

One of Saul's soldiers came and got the spear.
Saul went his way, and David went his way.
Saul and David never saw each other again.

THE LAME PRINCE

Saul never did catch David.
The Philistines attacked in many places.
Saul had to save his people.
He had to fight for them.
Saul and Jonathan led the army
against the Philistines.
The Philistines were too strong.
Saul's army was beaten.
Saul and Jonathan died in battle.
They died, fighting the Philistine soldiers.

David and his soldiers drove the Philistines away.
The people made David king of Israel.
"Long live King David," they shouted.

Mephibosheth sat in his room.
He was lame.
He could not walk at all.
He could not join the people.
"I am glad King David does not know me,"
he thought.
"Prince Jonathan, my father,
and King Saul, my grandfather, are dead.
They died fighting the Philistines.
And who is the new king of Israel?
Saul's enemy, David.
David, the enemy of my grandfather,
is the new king of Israel.
I am glad he does not know me."

Knock, knock.
Someone knocked on the door.

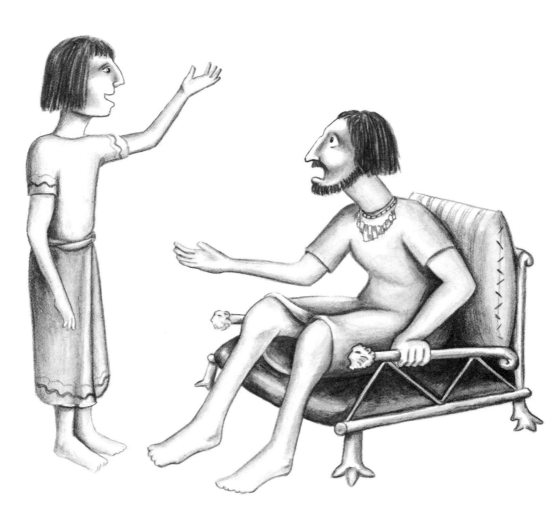

"Who is there?" called Mephibosheth.
"Ziba is here.
Ziba, your servant.
Ziba has good news for you."
"Come in," called Mephibosheth.
"Master, master," said Ziba,
"I bring wonderful news.
King David wishes to see you."
"I thought that King David did not know me,"
said Mephibosheth.

"David was the enemy of my grandfather, Saul.
What can David want with me?
He may harm me.
No, I will not go.
I will stay here.
I am lame in both feet.
I cannot run away, I cannot even walk.
I am safer here."

"King David will not harm you.
He wants to help you.
David and your father, Prince Jonathan,
were good friends.
Jonathan saved David's life.
And David has not forgotten.

"Come. I will take you to the king.
He wants to give you all your grandfather's land
and all the things that belonged to Saul.
He wants you to eat at his royal table.
He wants to take care of you."
"Oh, Ziba," said Mephibosheth.
"David must be a wonderful man
and a wonderful friend.
He forgets that my grandfather was his enemy.
But he remembers that my father was his friend.
Take me to the king, Ziba.
And let me shout with all the people,
'Long live King David.'"

WHO WILL BE KING?

King David had many sons.
They were all princes in Israel.
They all wanted to be king, after their father.
David trusted three men: Nathan, the prophet;
Zadok, the priest;
and Benanaiah, the captain of the guard.

One day, David said to Nathan,
"The next king of Israel must be my son Solomon."
"But Solomon is your youngest son.
He is only a boy," said Nathan.
"What will your other sons say?
Will they want Solomon to be king?
I am sure they will not.
Each one wants to be king himself."

"Solomon is my youngest,
but he will make the best king," said David.
"Ask him about anything.
Ask him about the animals, the flowers, the trees,
how cold winter wind becomes summer's warm breeze.
Ask him how the stars can show
tired travelers where to go.
Ask Solomon any question at all.
He will answer it.
He must be the next king.
We will make sure of that.

"This is my plan.
You, Nathan, with Benanaiah and Zadok,
will find Solomon now.

Put him on my royal mule.
Lead him through the streets of Jerusalem,
all the way to the spring of Gihon.
At the spring of Gihon, anoint Solomon, bless him,
and proclaim him the next king of Israel."

That is just what those three men did.
They found Solomon.
They sat him on the king's mule.
They led him through the streets of Jerusalem
to the spring of Gihon.
At the spring, Zadok said, "Solomon, son of David,
get off your mule and come to me."

Solomon got off the mule.
He stood straight and tall before Zadok.
"Solomon, son of David, as chief priest
of the God of Israel,
I anoint you the next king of Israel," said Zadok.

And he put some holy oil on Solomon's head.
"Listen to the voice of God and the commandments.
Then you will be a good leader, loved by your people,
and happy in everything you do."

The soldiers blew their *shofarot*.
And everyone shouted, "Long live King Solomon."

SOLOMON'S WISH

Solomon became king of Israel after David.
"Please settle our quarrels," said his people.
"King Solomon has a special gift,"
they said to each other.
"He has an understanding heart.
He is very wise.
He can settle our quarrels better than we can."

How did Solomon receive this gift?
One day, he made a special prayer.
"O *Adonai*," he prayed.
"Bless me and bless my kingdom.
There are so many problems.
I am like a little child.
I need Your help.
Please help me to help my people."

When he had finished,
Solomon felt God speaking to him.
"Solomon, I wish to give you a gift.
What gift shall I give you?"
"O *Adonai*," answered Solomon, "give me
an understanding heart, so I can tell good from evil
and make my people strong and happy."

"Solomon, Solomon," he felt God answer,
"most men ask gifts for themselves.
You do not.
You do not ask for money.
You do not ask for a long life.
You ask only for wisdom
to make your people strong and happy.

You shall have wisdom.
And, because you did not pray for yourself alone,
I shall give you other gifts.
You shall have children and grandchildren
to make your life happy."

Solomon lived to be a grandfather.
He built the most beautiful Temple in the whole world.
He built palaces
that visitors came from all over to see.
He could answer everyone's questions.
People said he was the wisest person
in the whole world.
Solomon wrote many of the proverbs in our Bible,
in the book we call the Book of Proverbs.

69

A ROYAL VISITOR

"Solomon is wiser than anyone in Israel,"
said the Hebrews.
"Solomon is the wisest person I know,"
said Hiram, king of Tyre.
"Solomon is the wisest person in the world,"
said the Pharaoh of Egypt.

"I don't believe these stories.
How can one person be so wise?"
thought the Queen of Sheba.
"I will find out for myself.
I will go to Jerusalem and see."

She called her servants.
"Prepare a camel train," she said.
"Load it with spices, precious stones,
and much fine gold.

Think up hard questions,"
she said to the wise people in her court.
"I am going to visit King Solomon.
I shall ask him many questions.
Then we shall see how wise he is."

That very day, the queen, her camel train,
and her wisest people set out for Jerusalem.
Solomon met the Queen of Sheba
at the gate of Jerusalem.
"I am happy to have such a beautiful visitor,"
he said.
"And I am happy to have such a wise host,"
said the queen.
"People say you are the wisest person in the world.
I did not believe them.
I came to find out for myself.
I came with a long list of questions.
I am sure nobody can answer them all;
but maybe you will try."
"I shall be delighted," said Solomon.

The Queen of Sheba asked questions
all that day,
and all the next,
and all the day after that.
She asked Solomon questions
until she could not think of any more questions to ask.
And, for every question, Solomon had the answer.
"I have traveled far," said the queen.
"But you are indeed the wisest person I have ever met.
You must be the wisest person in the world."

SOLOMON'S TEMPLE

King David did many things for his people.
He conquered the Philistines.
He made Israel a strong country
and Jerusalem the capital city.

King David always wanted to build a temple to God.
"We need a place to keep the Holy Ark," said David.
"We need a special place where we can worship God."

David never built this temple,
but his dream came true anyway.

His son made his dream come true.
His son, Solomon, built the Temple.
Thousands of people helped Solomon.
For seven years they worked.
They cut huge stone blocks
to make the Temple walls.
They cut down tremendous cedar trees
to make the inside walls.
Artists dipped brushes in gold paint
to decorate the inside walls of the Temple.

When the work was finished,
Solomon called his people together.
"My father, King David, wanted to build
a house for God," he said.
"God said to him, 'Your hands have made war
so you cannot build the house.
When your son, Solomon, grows up,
he will build it.'
I have made my father's dream come true.

I have built a house for God.
This house has a place for the Holy Ark
and a special place for the Ten Commandments.

"Blessed be *Adonai*, our God," said Solomon.
"May *Adonai* be with us as with our ancestors.
May we always remember our promise
to walk in God's ways, keep the commandments,
and never forget that only *Adonai* is the One God."

Hear, O Israel,	*Shema Yisrael*
The Lord is our God,	*Adonai Elohenu*
The Lord is One. Amen.	*Adonai Echad. Amen.*